WELCOME
to
DeLand, Florida

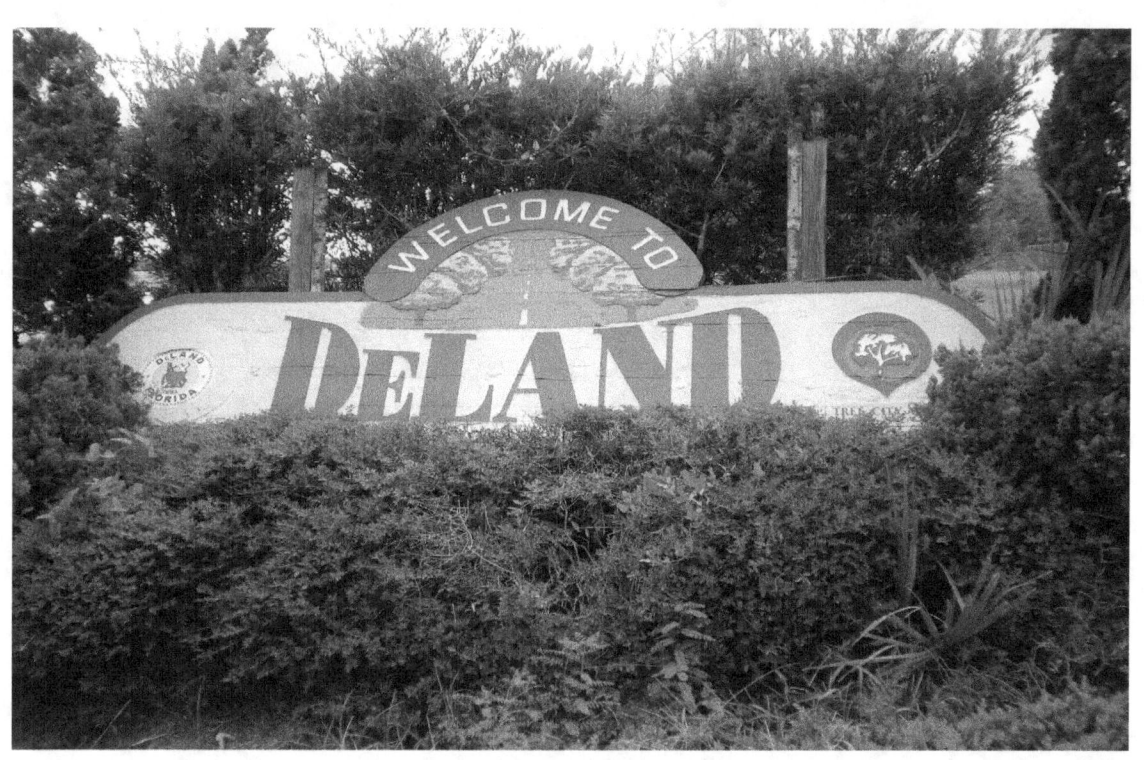

A beautiful little southern town.

By:

Bob Austin

Welcome to DeLand
A beautiful little southern town.

This is a collection of pictures that I have taken
around DeLand.

Without the support and encouragement
of my wonderful partner
Alan Austin
this would have never happened.

All photographs have been taken by
Bob Austin

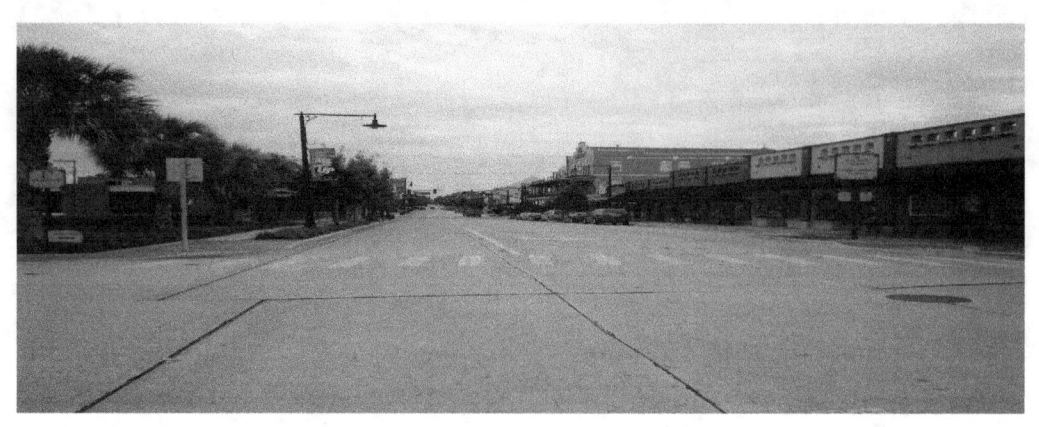

Looking up and down Main Street in downtown DeLand

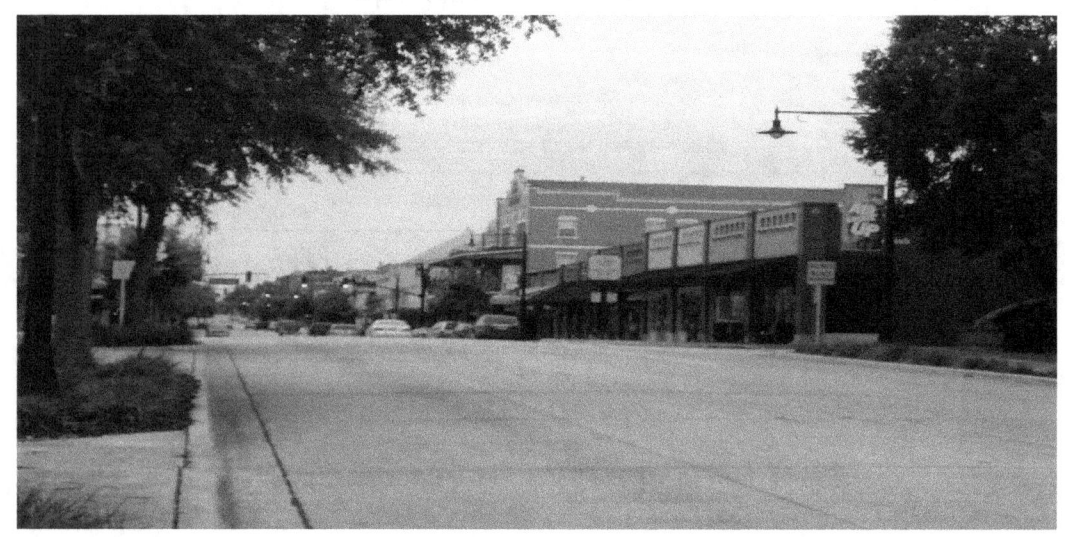

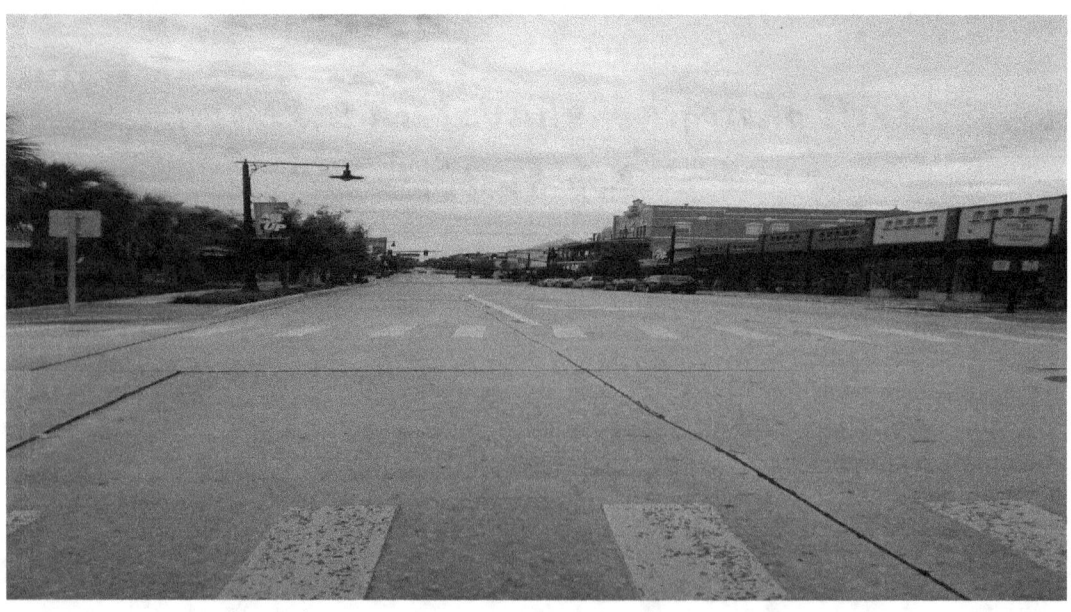

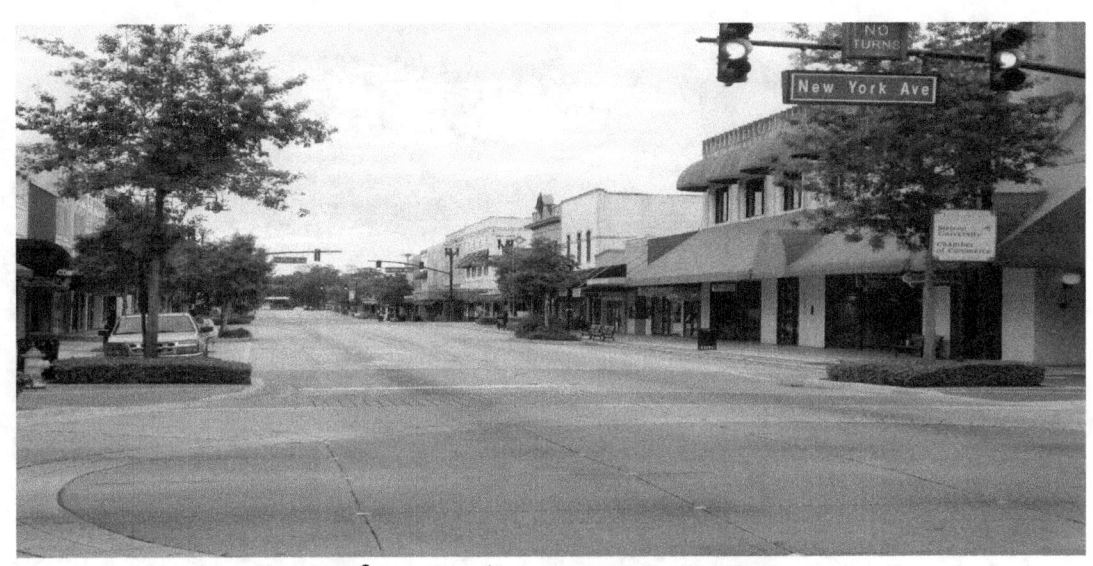

Another look at Main Street

The next 19 photos are of the painted Murial Walls of downtown DeLand.

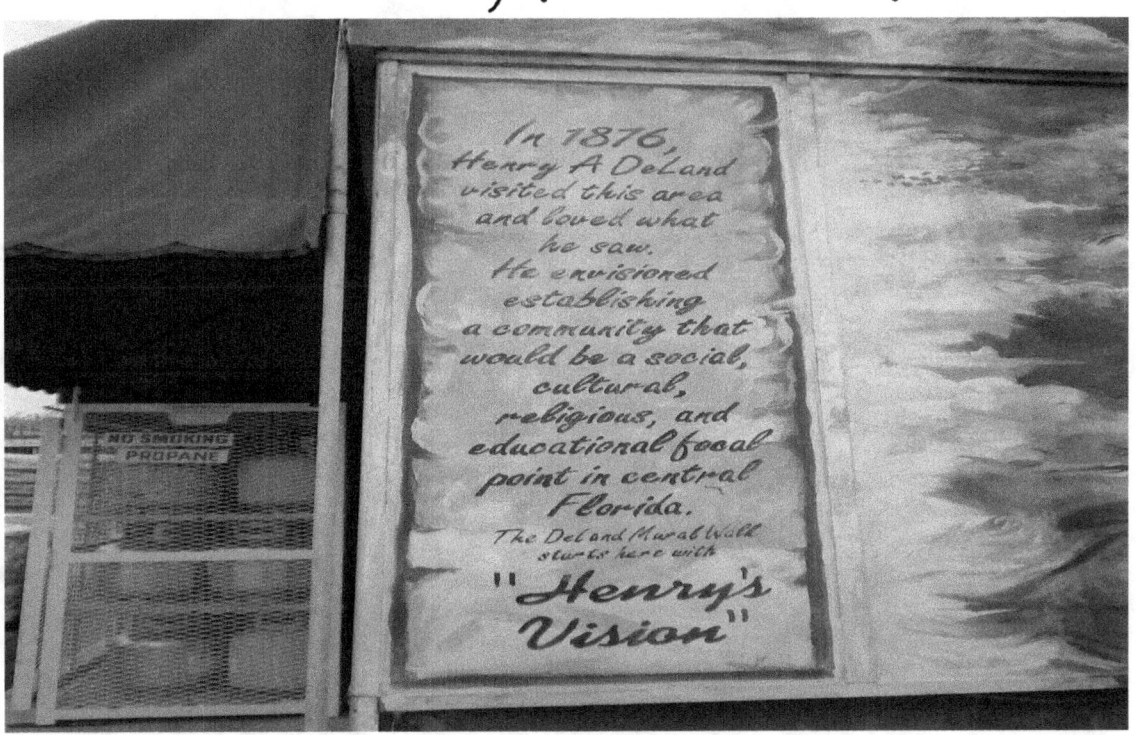

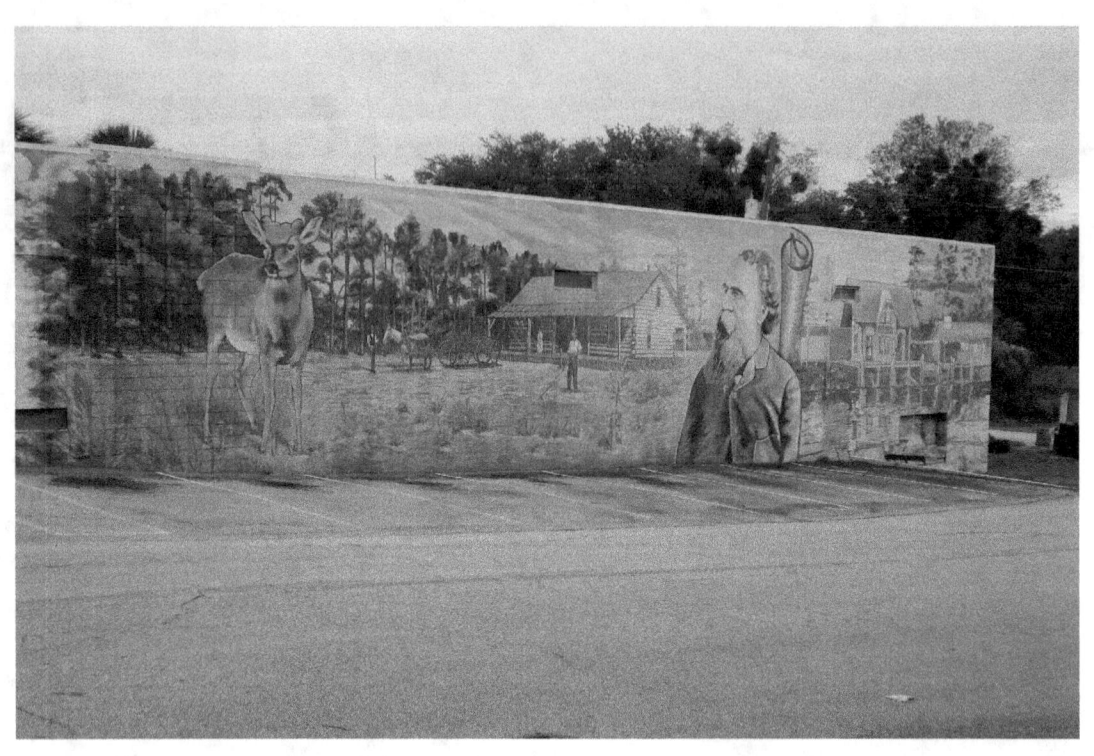

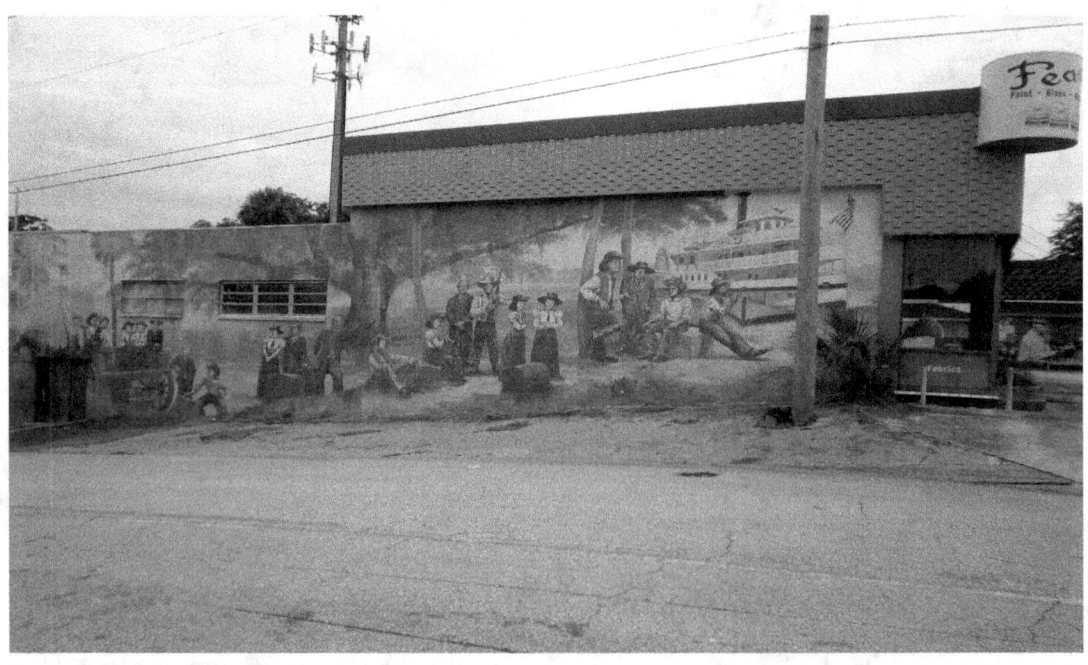

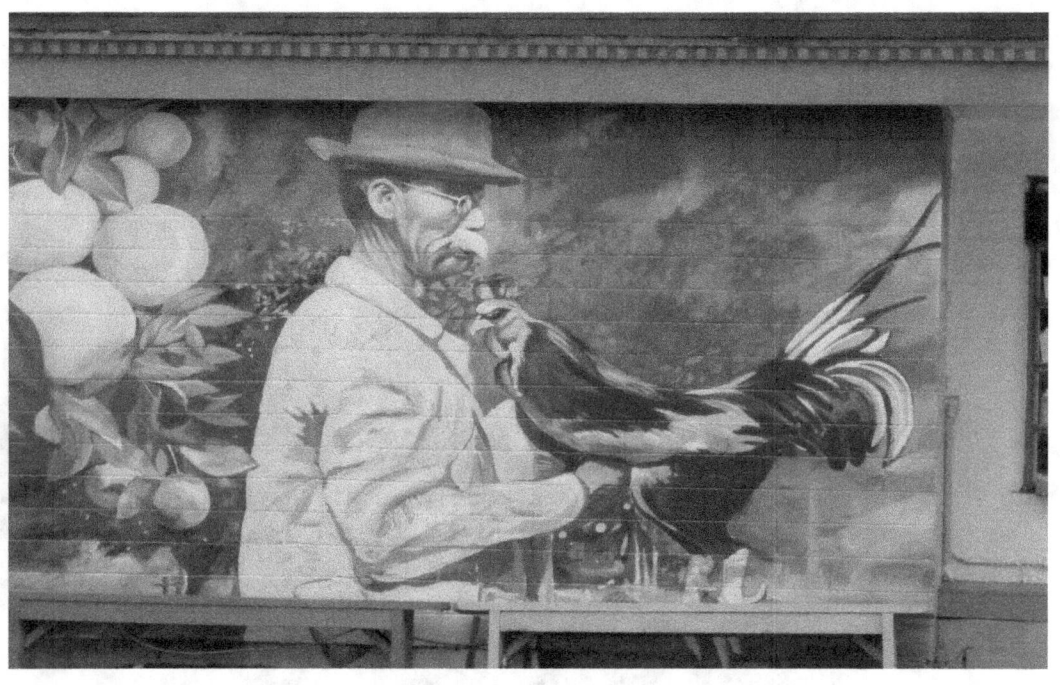

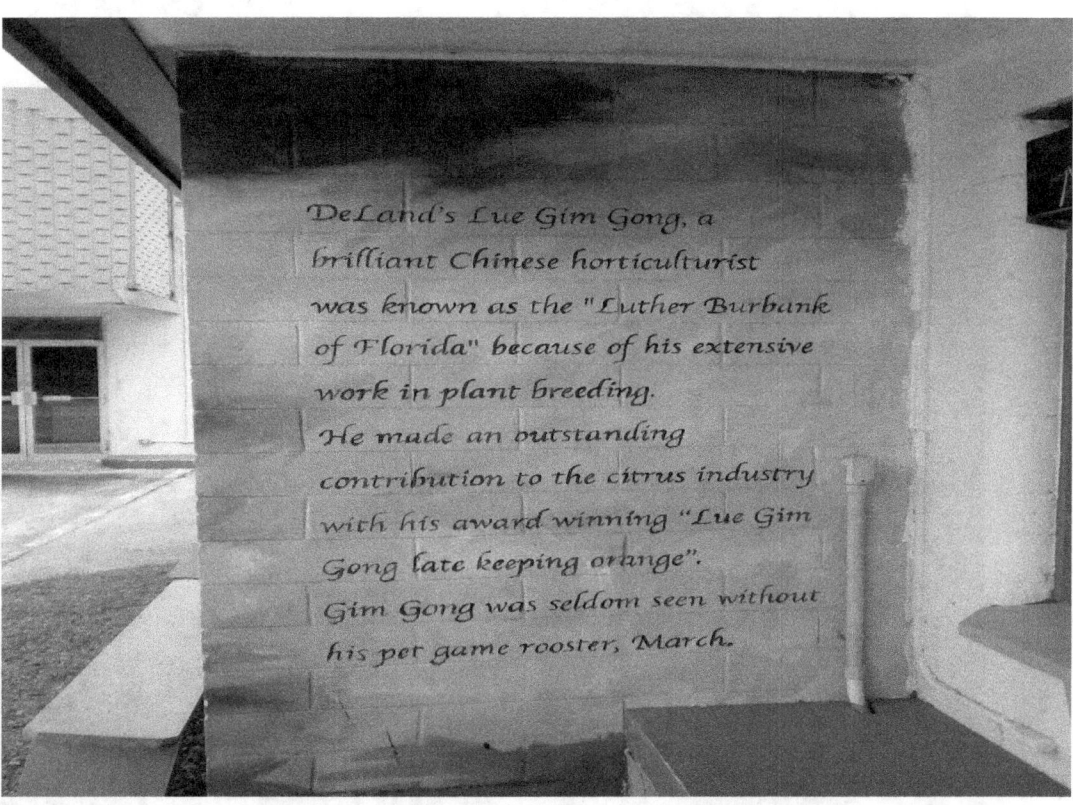

DeLand's Lue Gim Gong, a
brilliant Chinese horticulturist
was known as the "Luther Burbank
of Florida" because of his extensive
work in plant breeding.
He made an outstanding
contribution to the citrus industry
with his award winning "Lue Gim
Gong late keeping orange".
Gim Gong was seldom seen without
his pet game rooster, March.

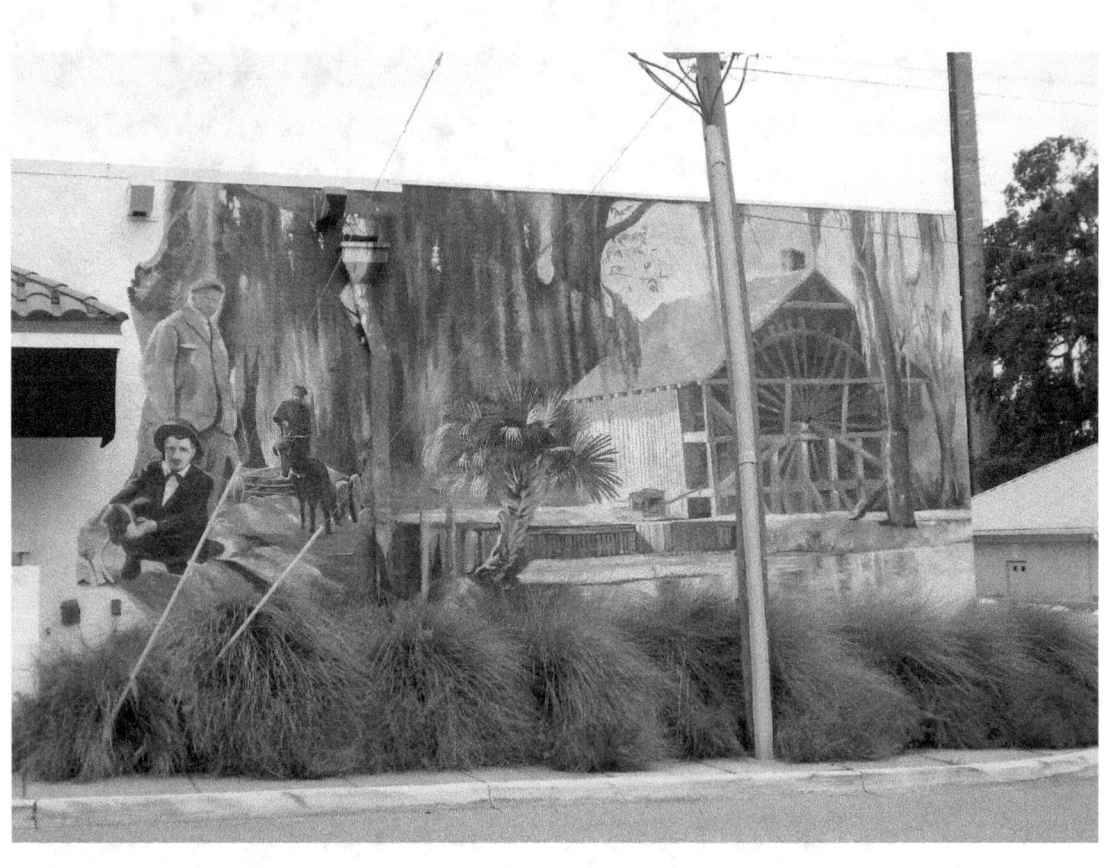

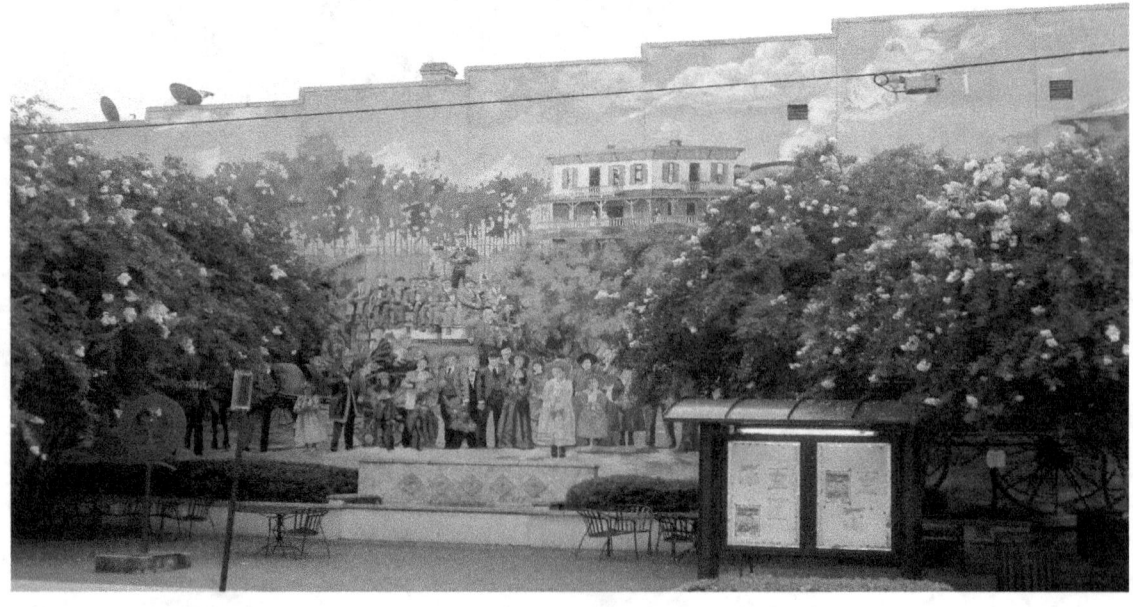

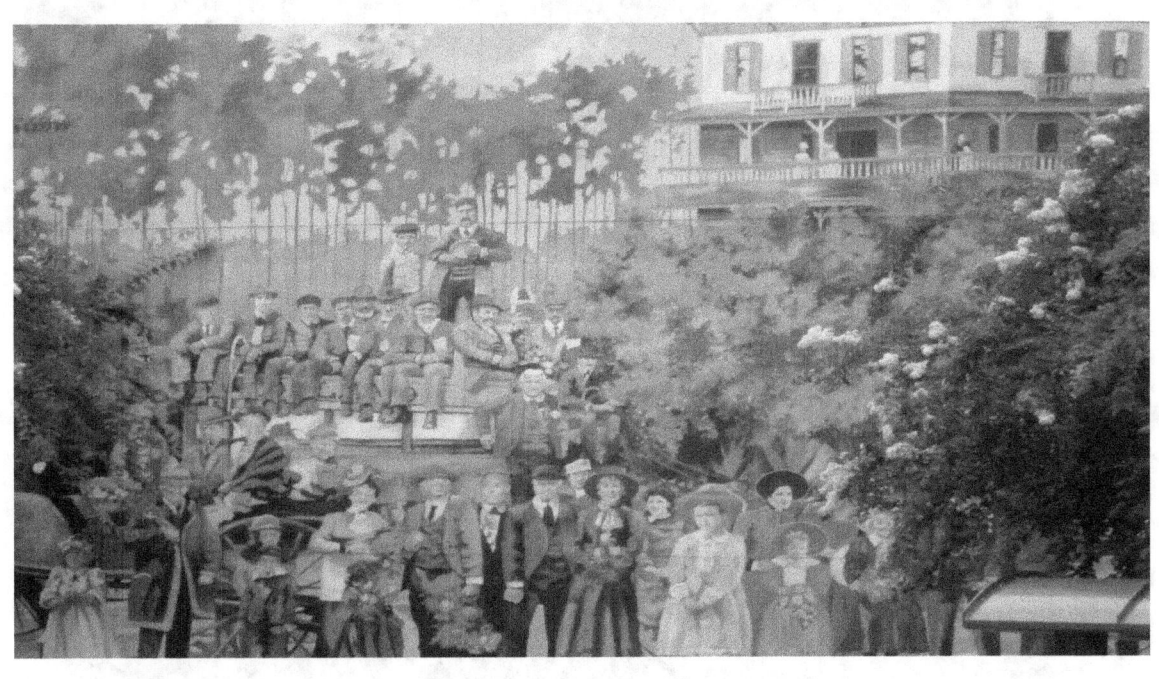

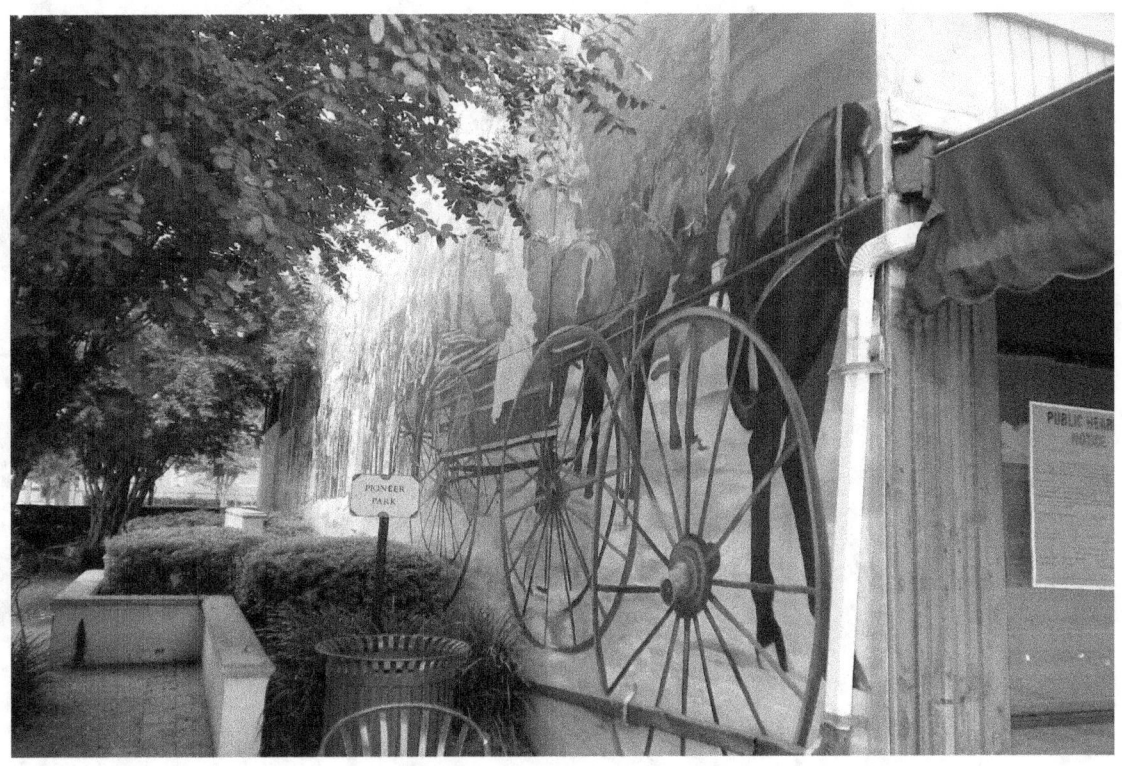

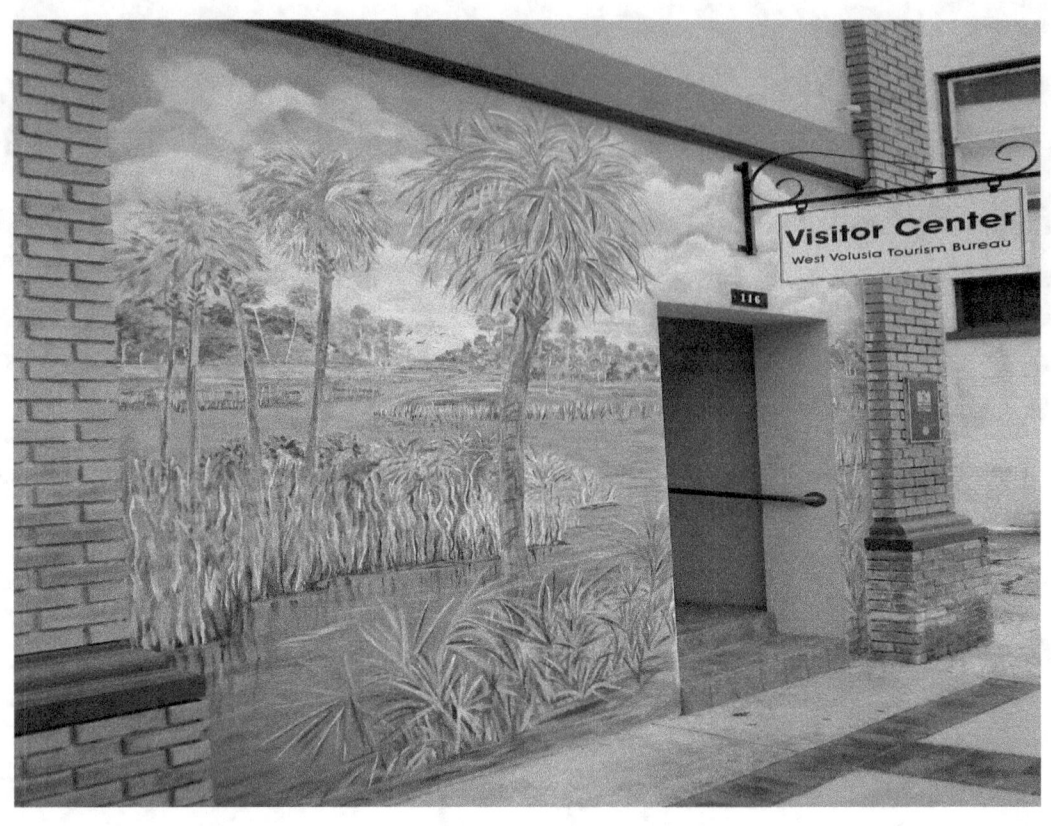

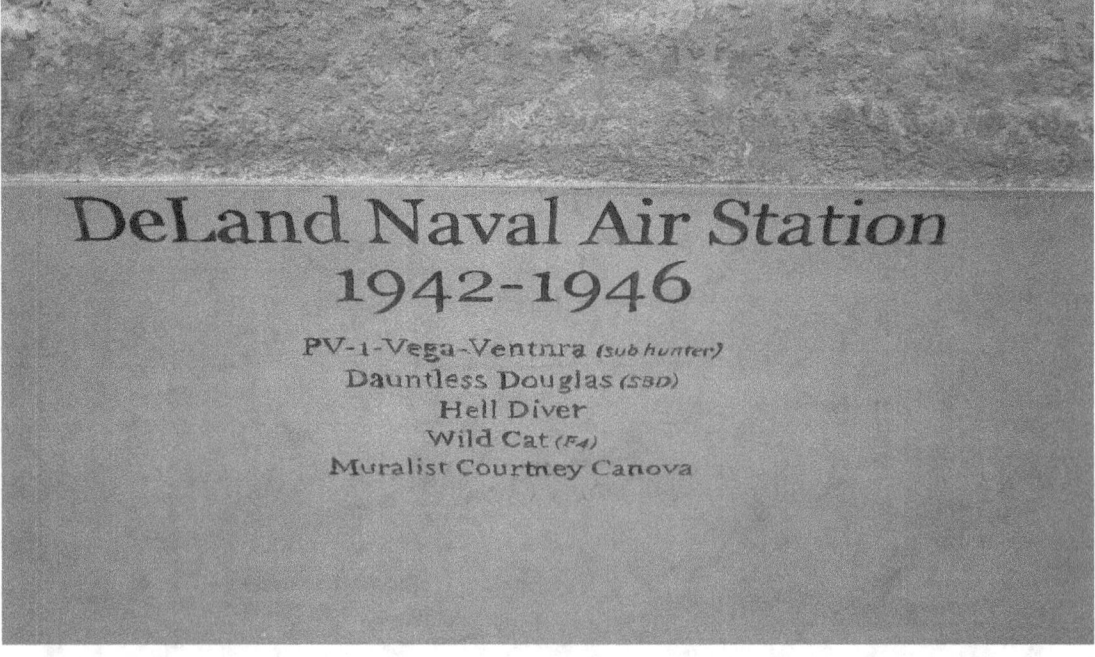

DeLand Naval Air Station
1942-1946

PV-1-Vega-Ventura (sub hunter)
Dauntless Douglas (SBD)
Hell Diver
Wild Cat (F4)
Muralist Courtney Canova

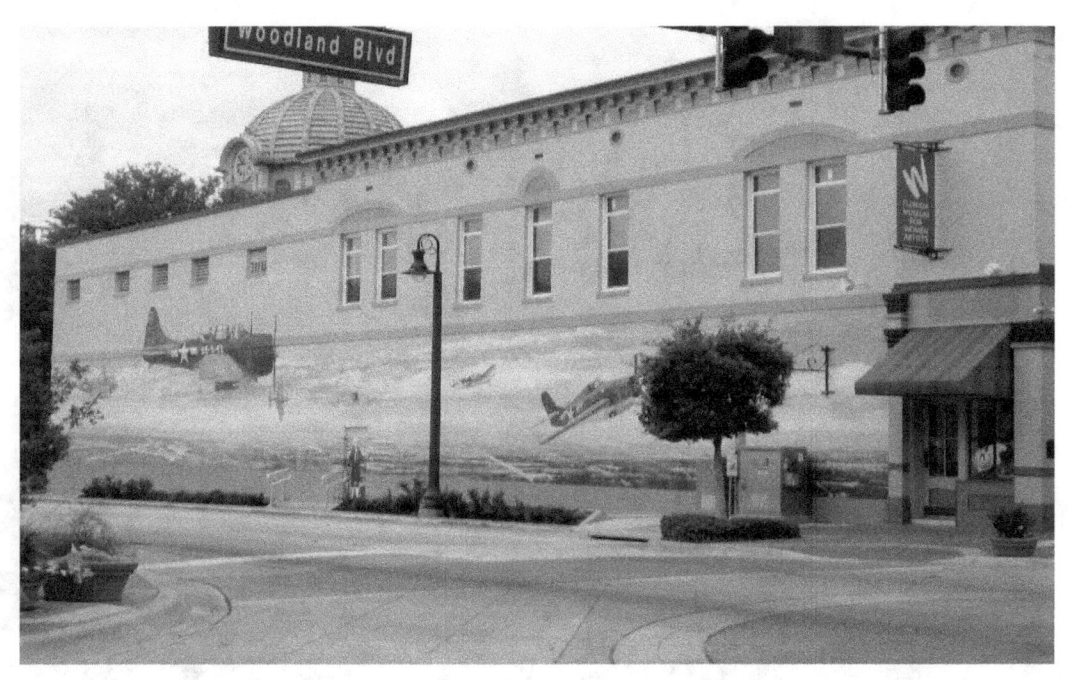

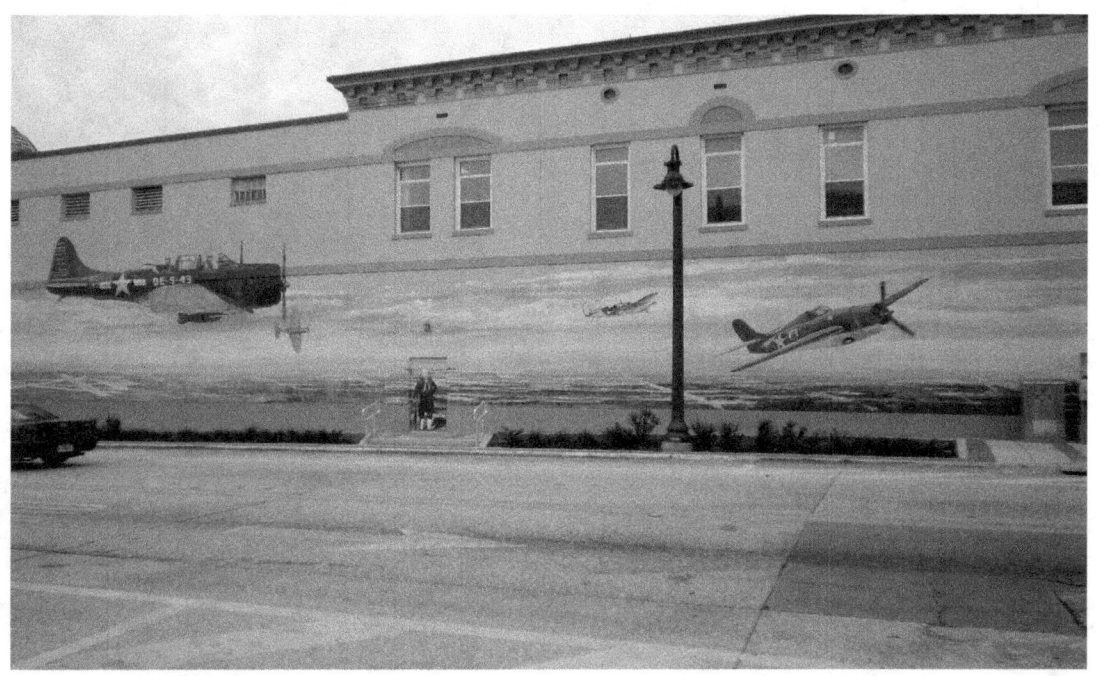

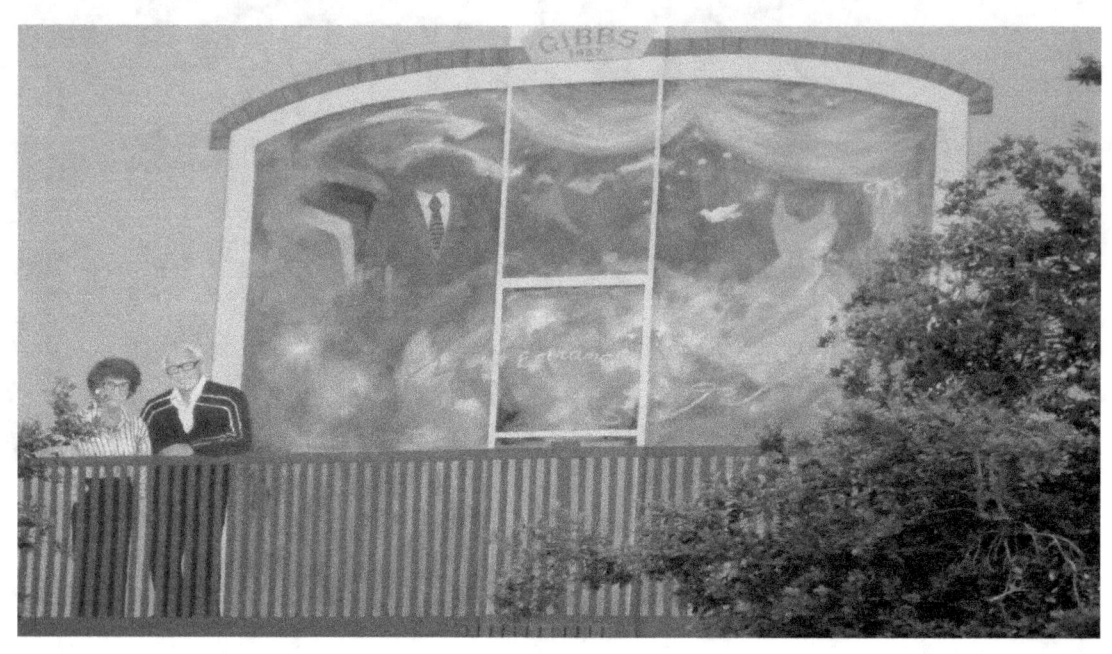

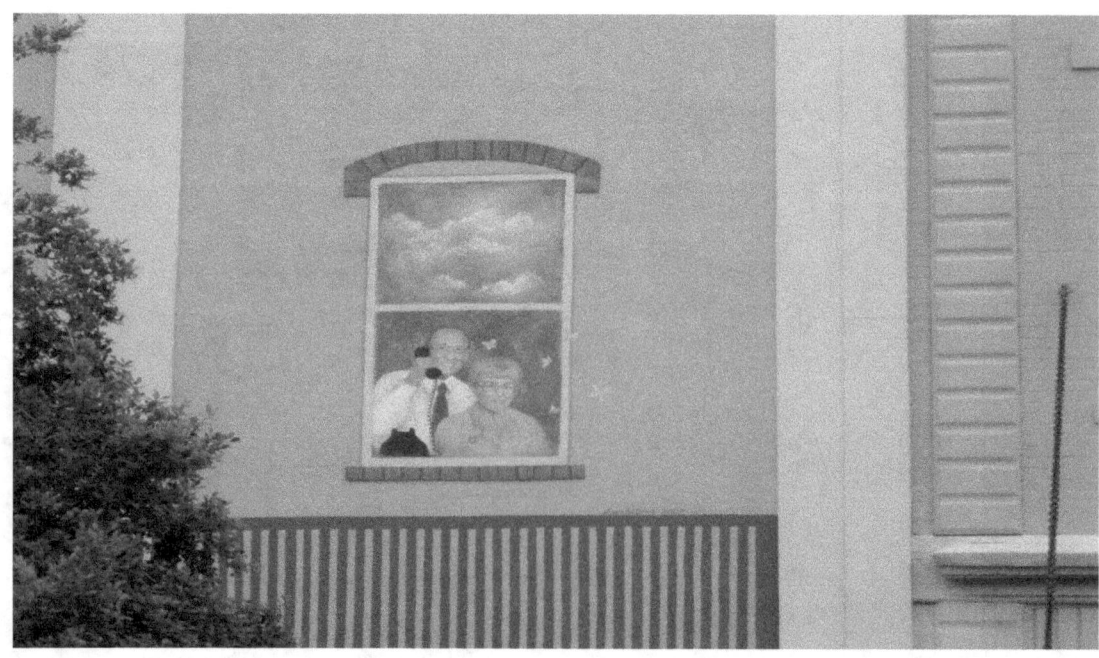

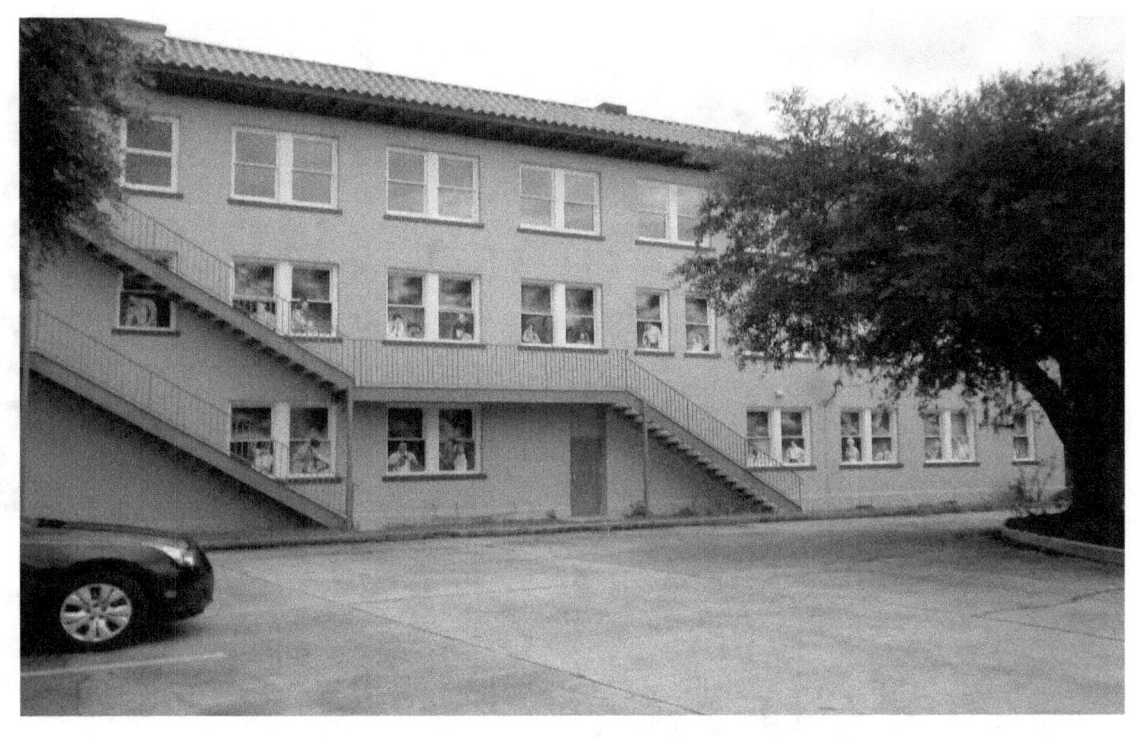

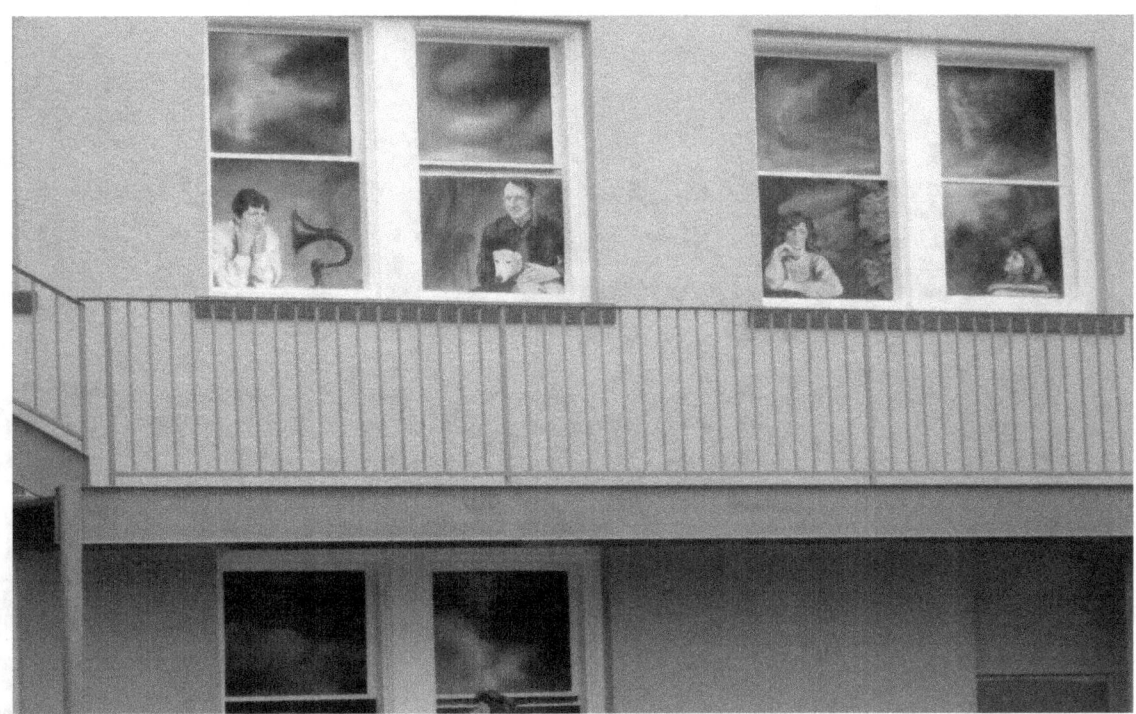

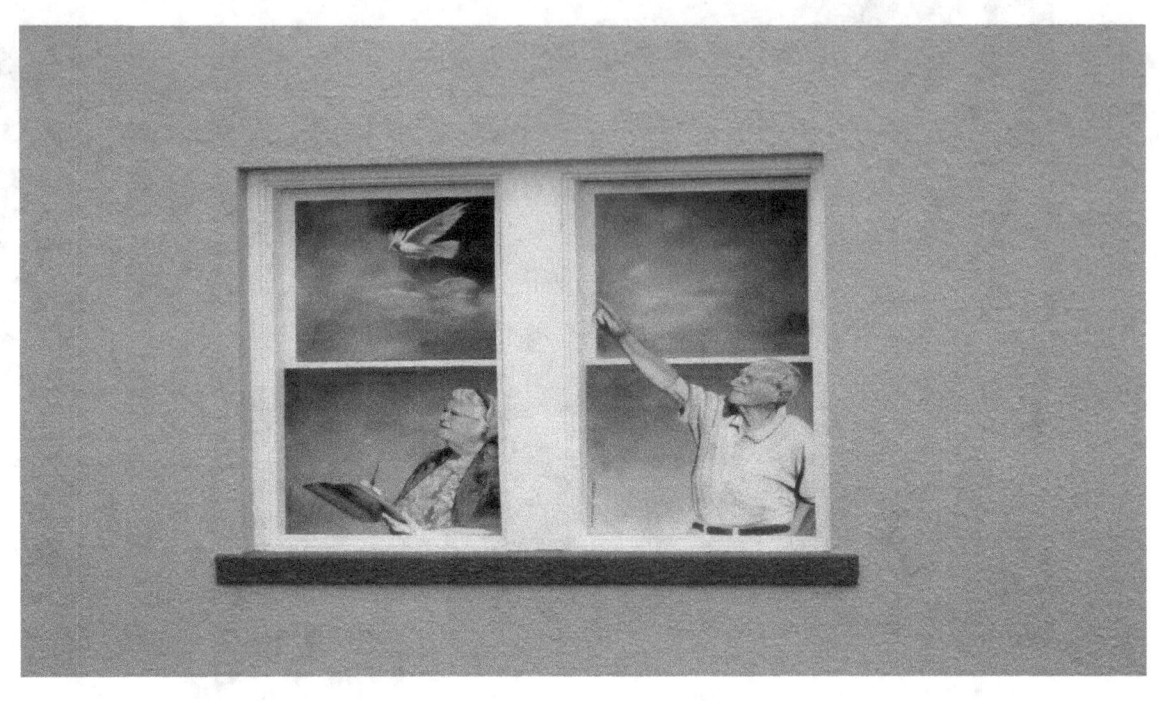

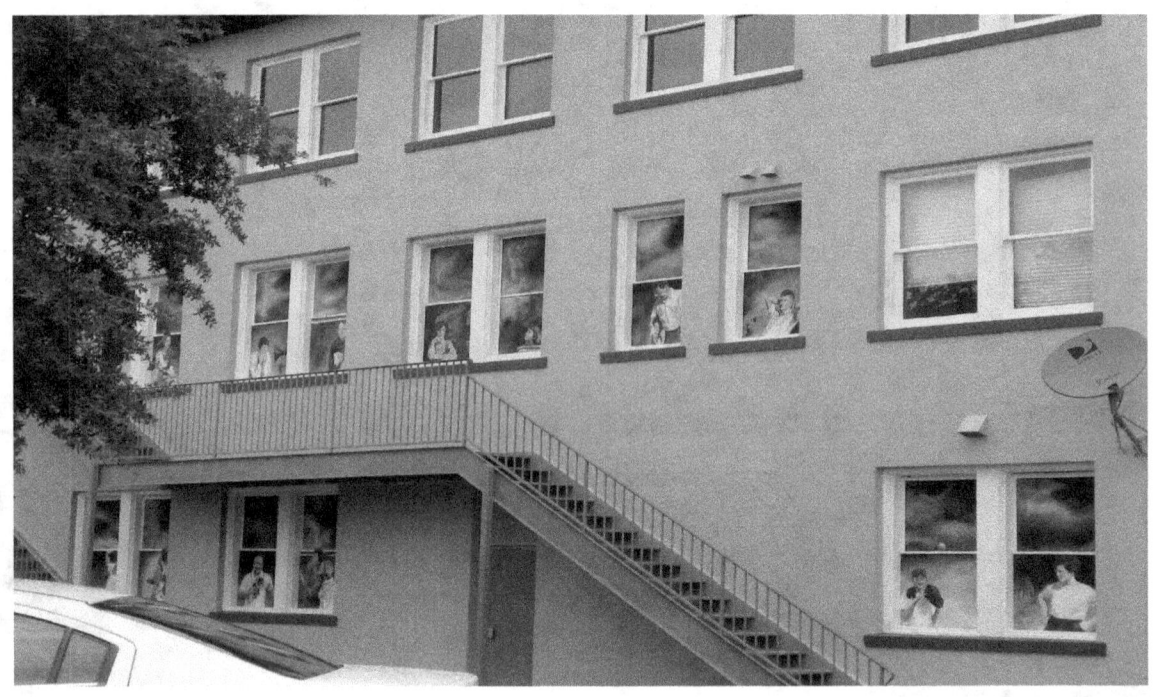

These 2 photos are of the old DeLand Opera House
built in 1910

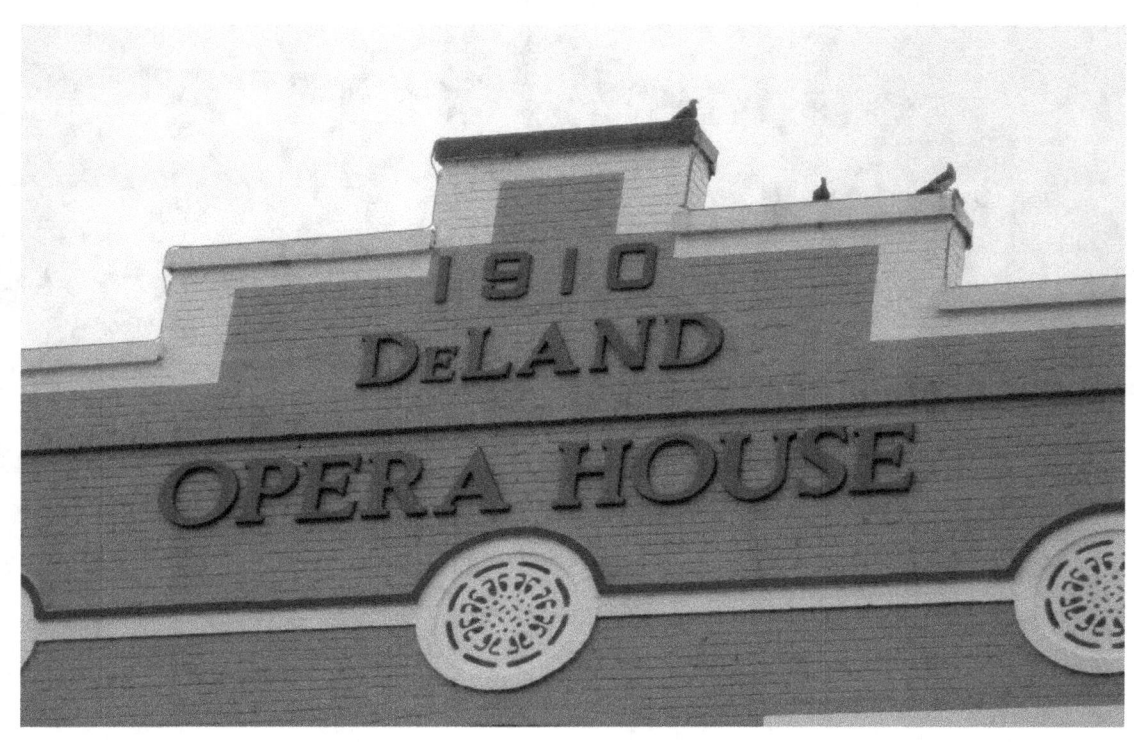

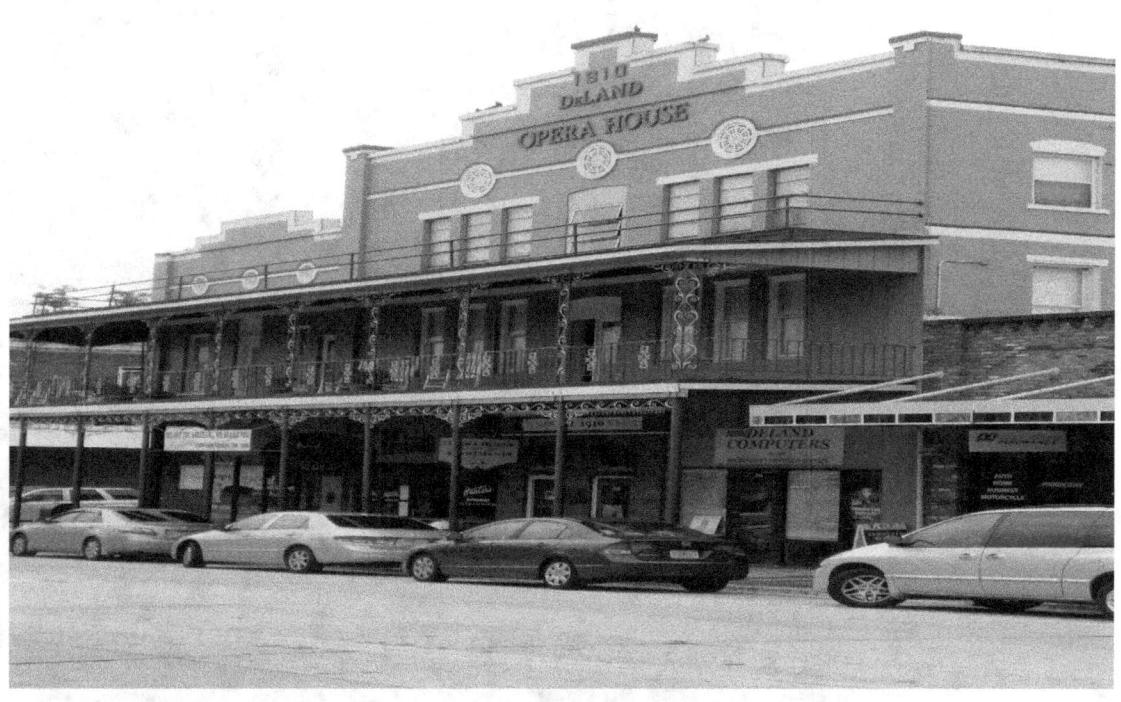

The next 2 photos are of the
Florida Museum For Women Artist

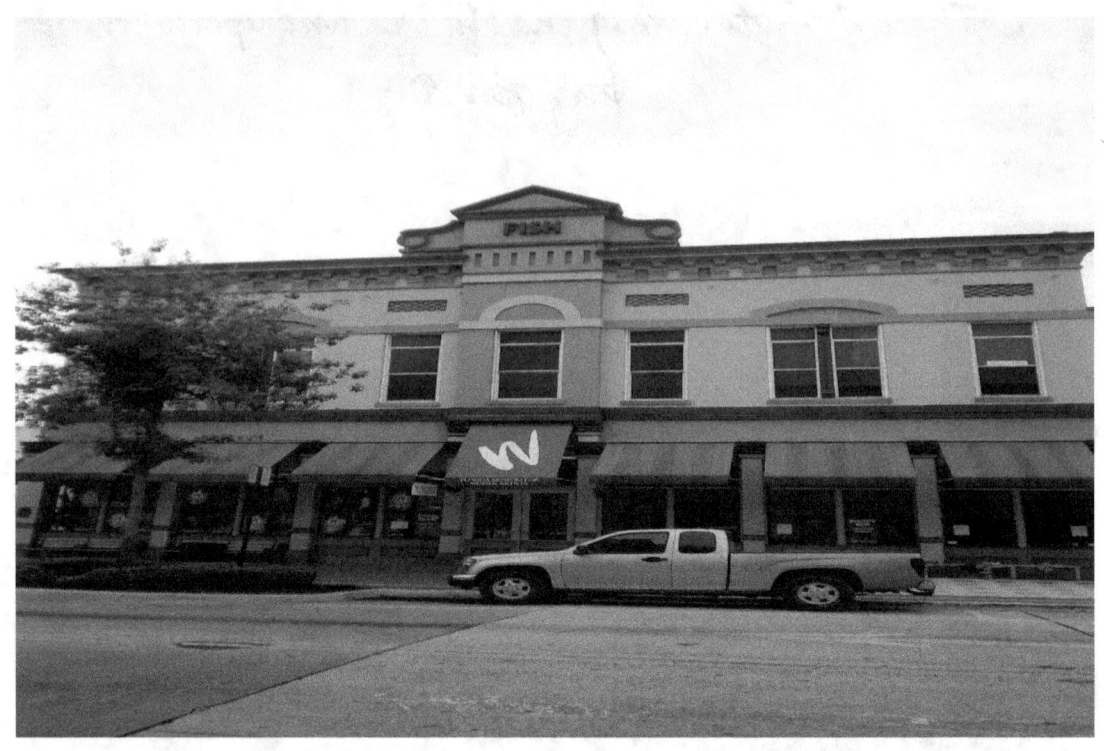

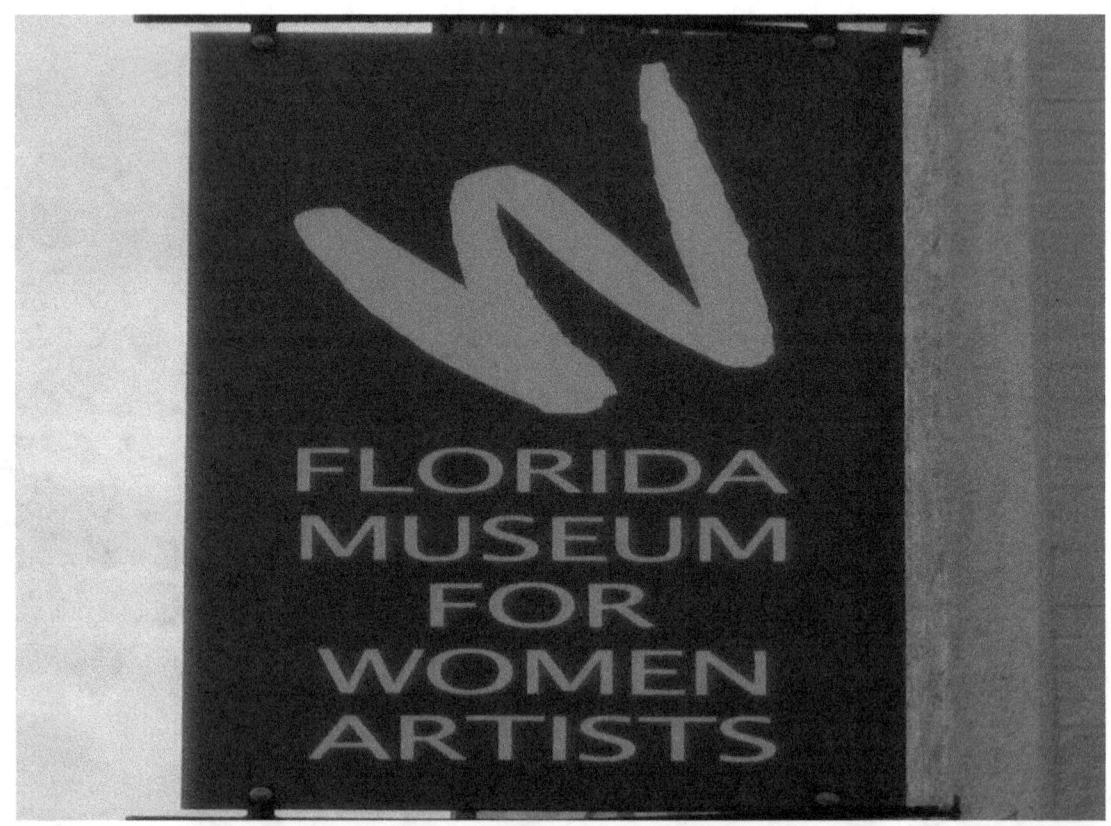

The next 2 photos are of the
Voluisa County Courthouse

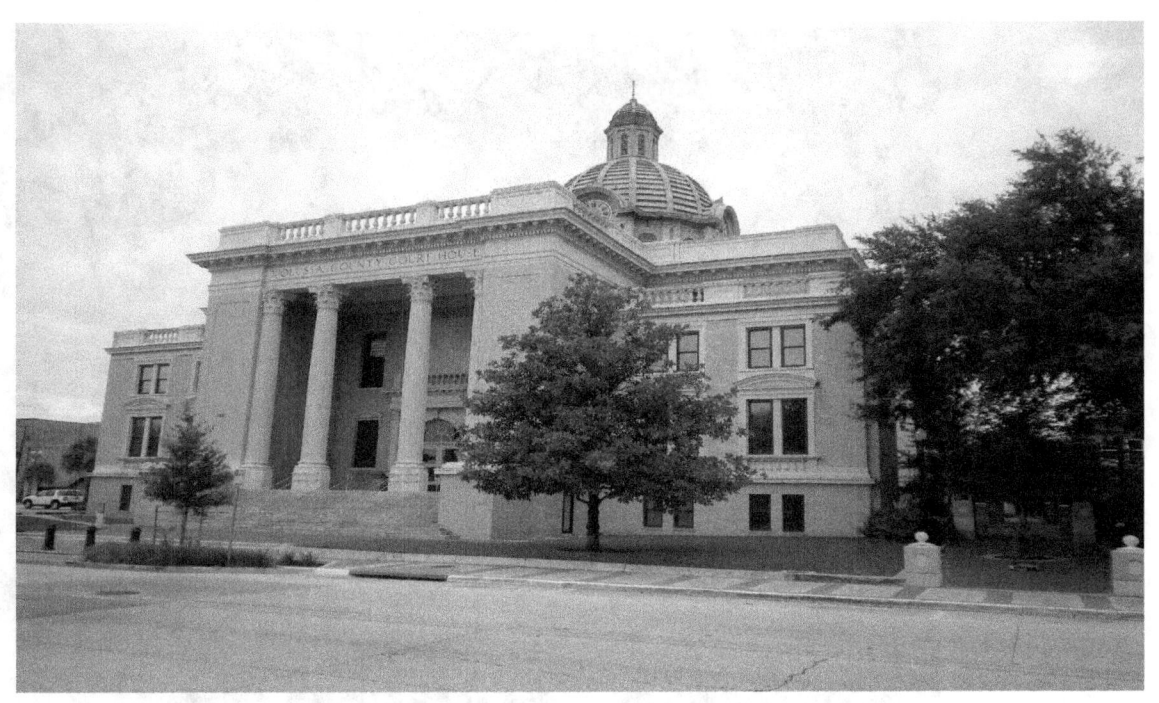

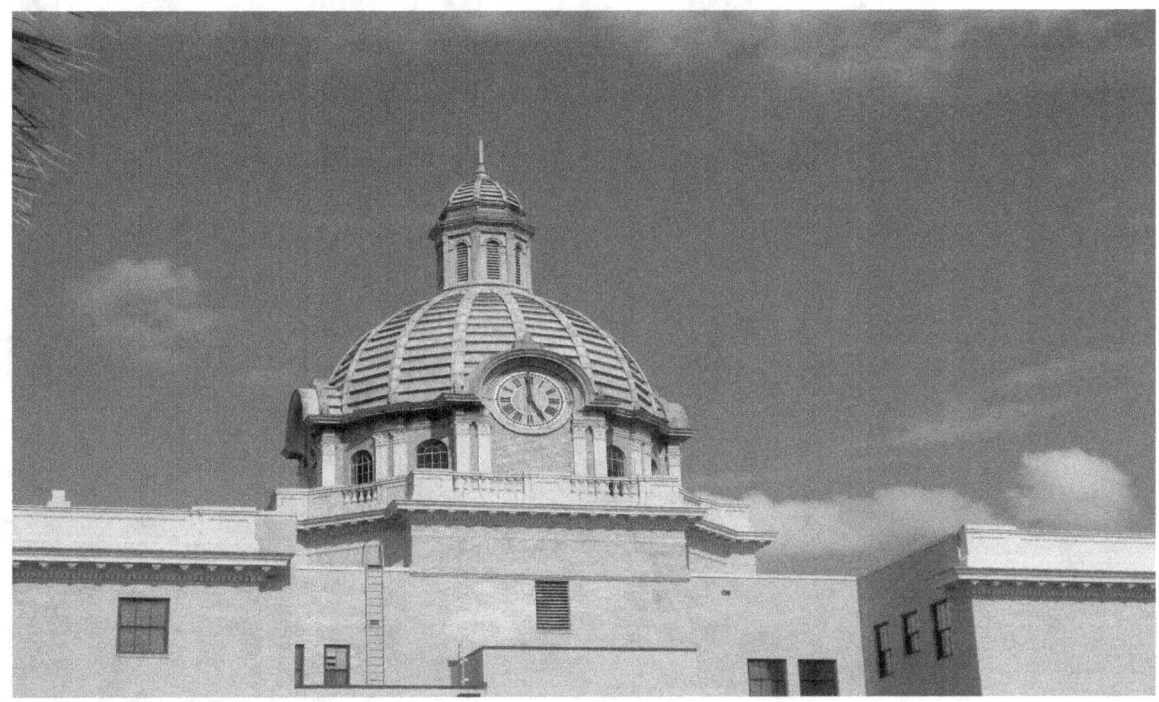

This is a photo of the sign for
the Garden District

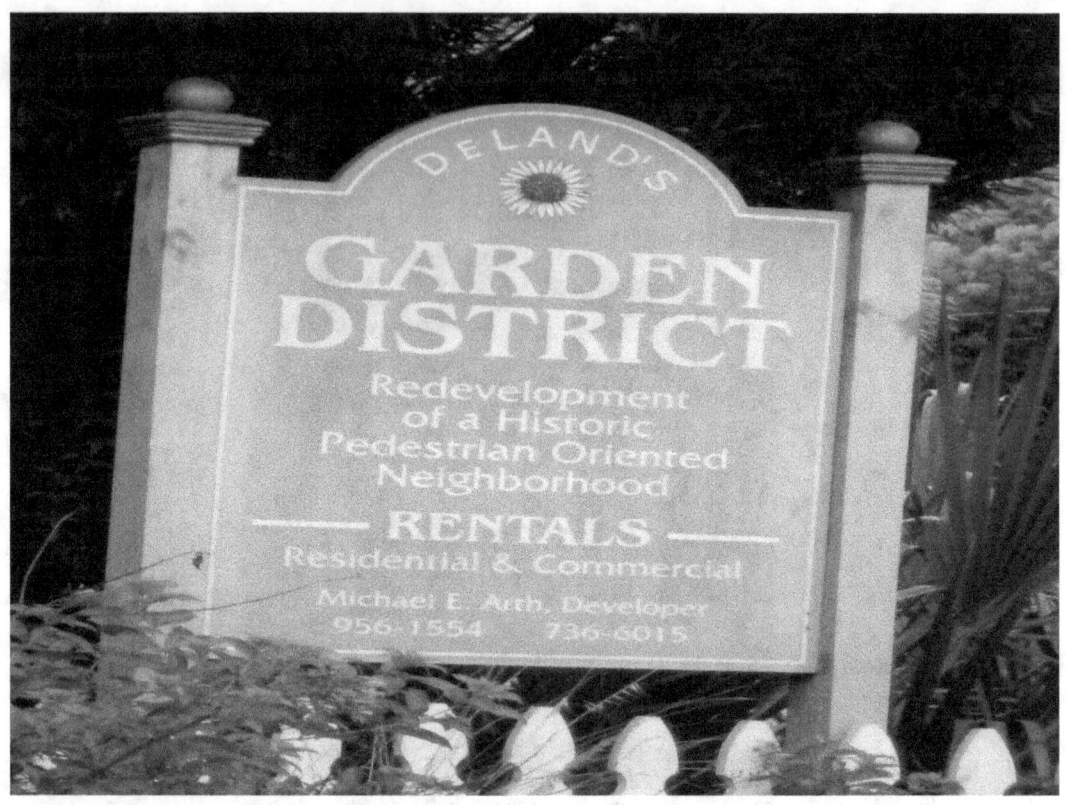

A moss covered tree (common here)

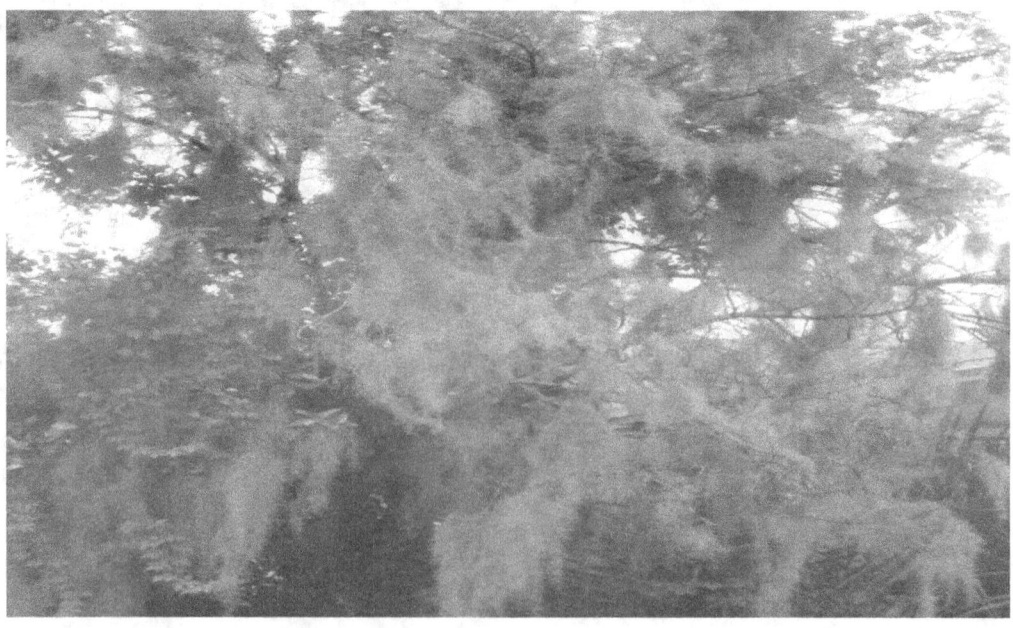

The Henry A. DeLand House
Mr. DeLand is the founder of DeLand

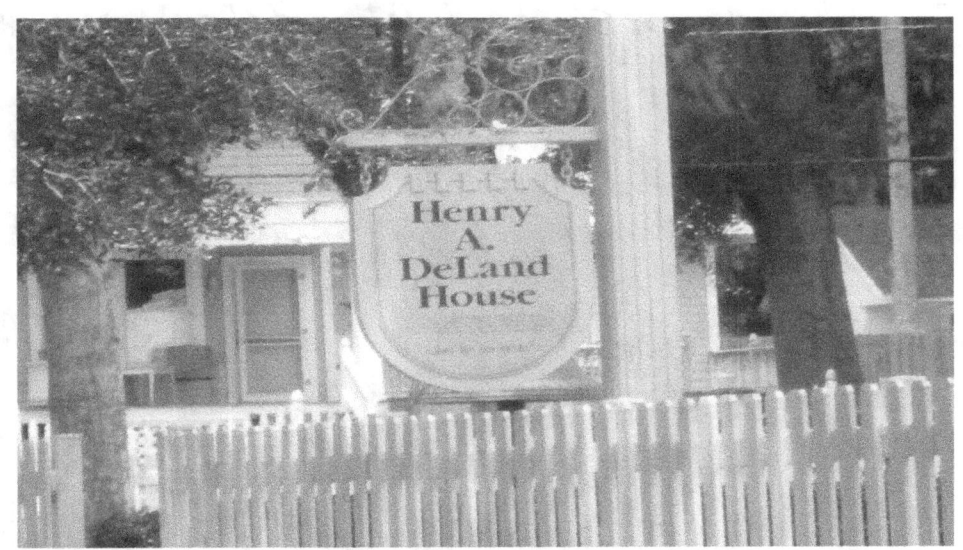

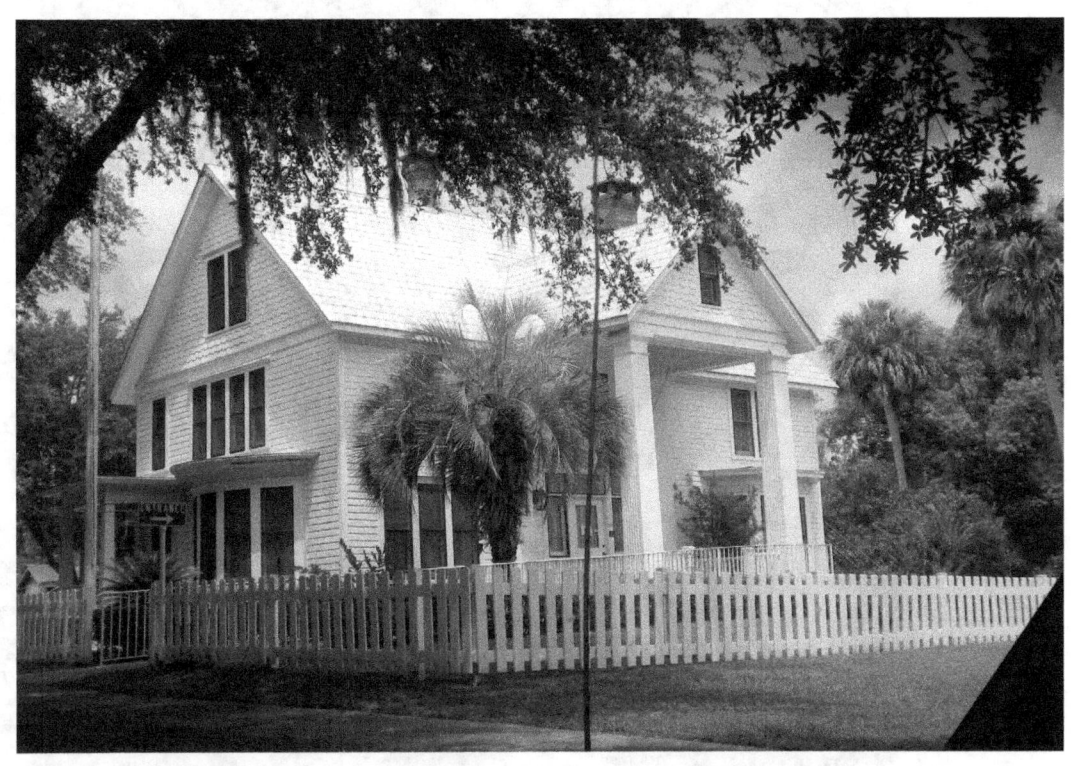

The next photos are of the
Steston Mansion
built by John B. Stetson, maker of the Stetson Hat.

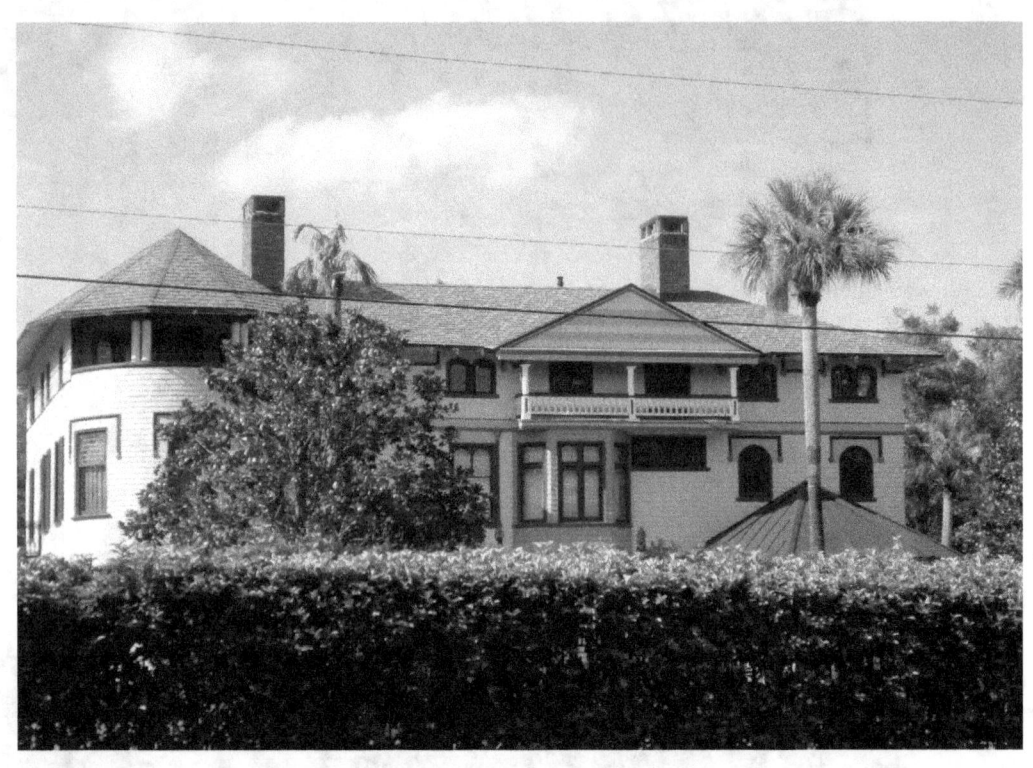

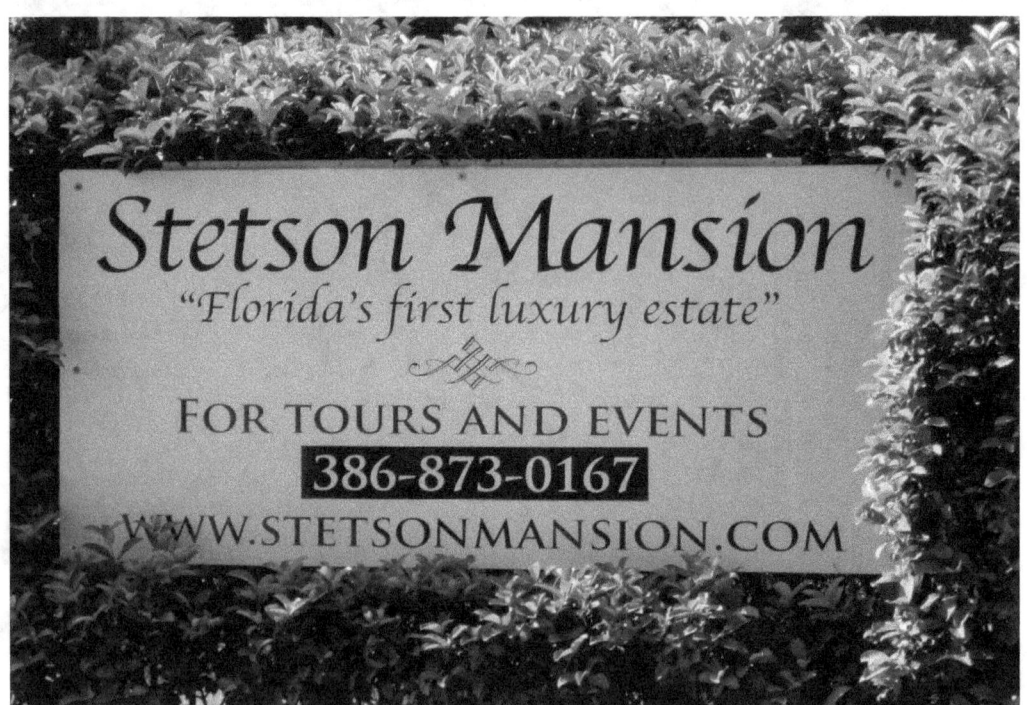

DeLand Airport

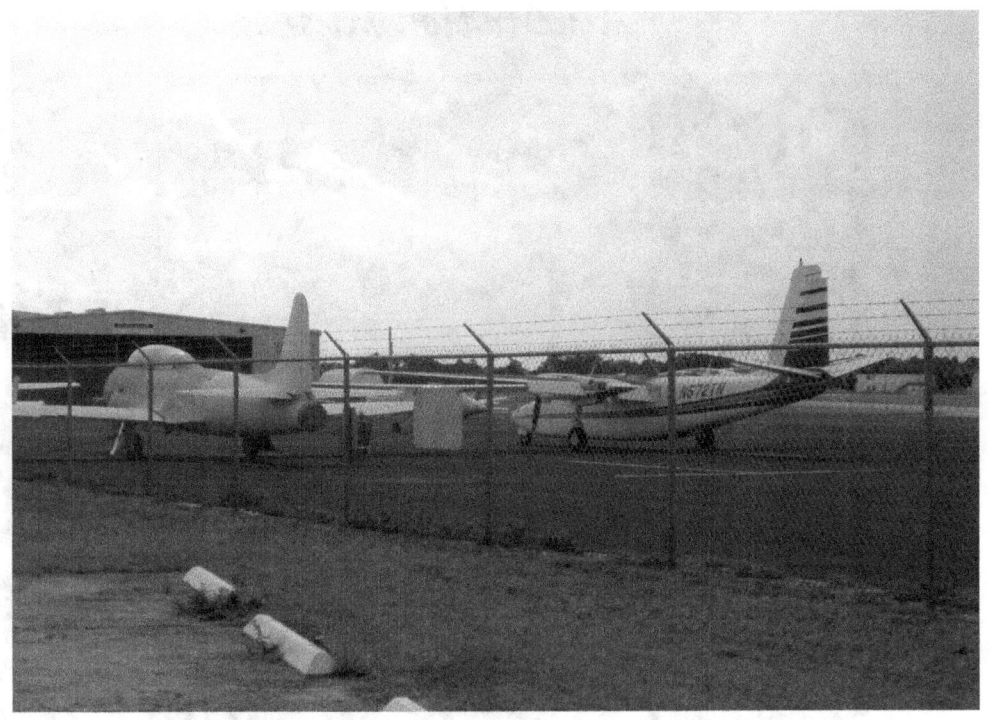

Skydive DeLand

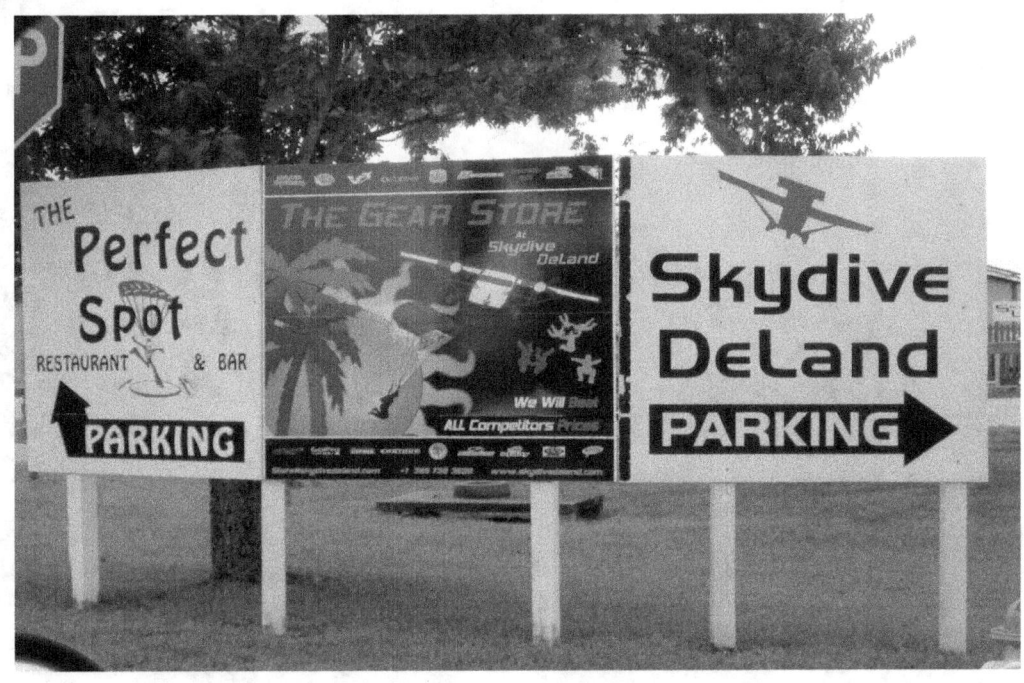

The DeLand Naval
Air Station Museum

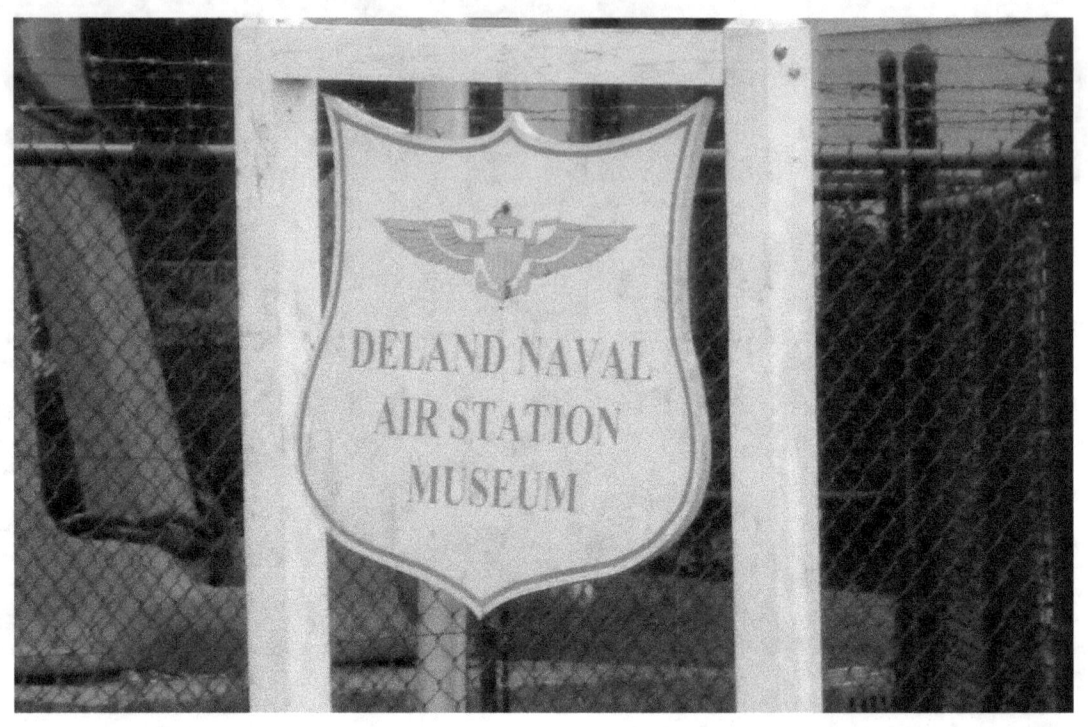

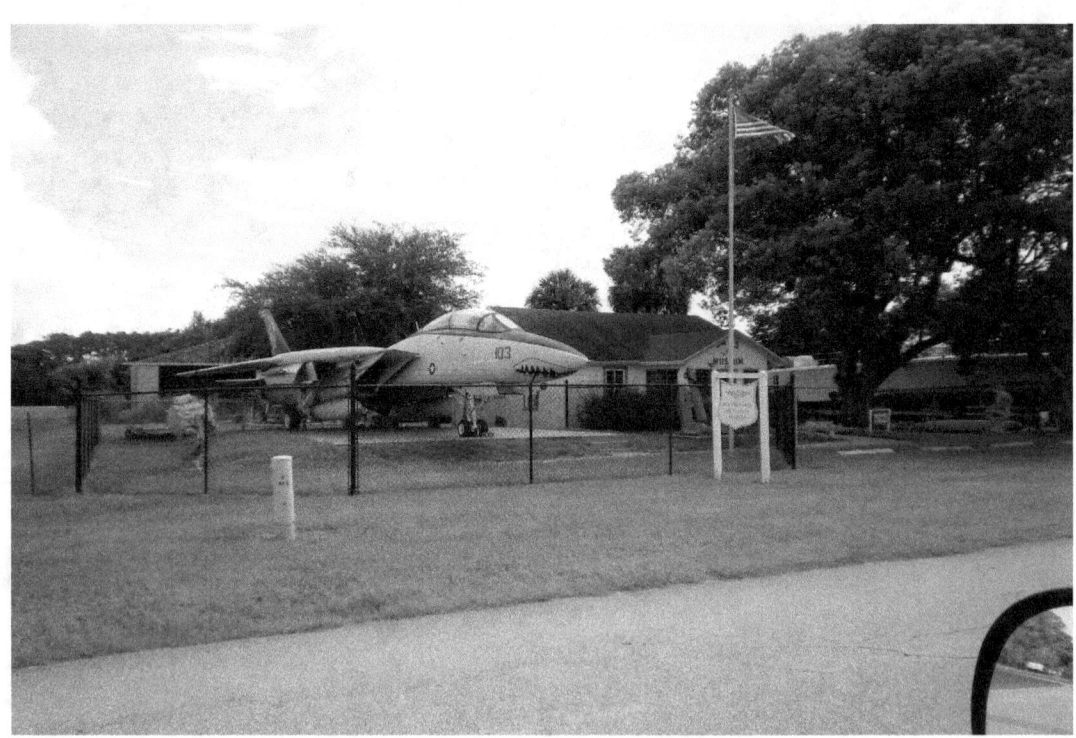

The Athens Theatre

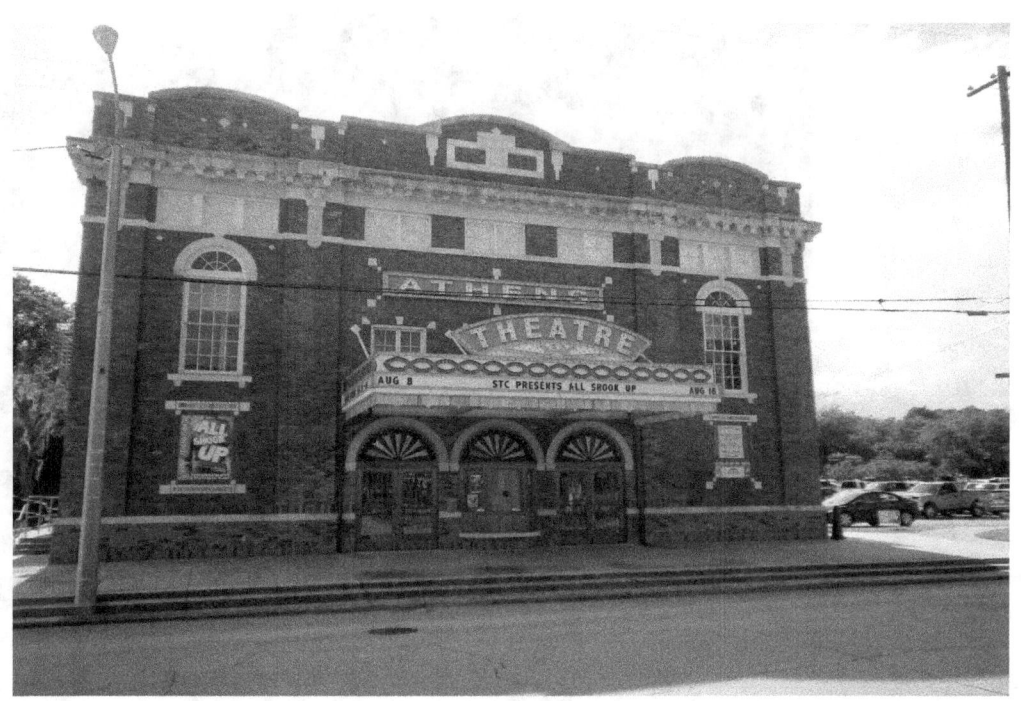

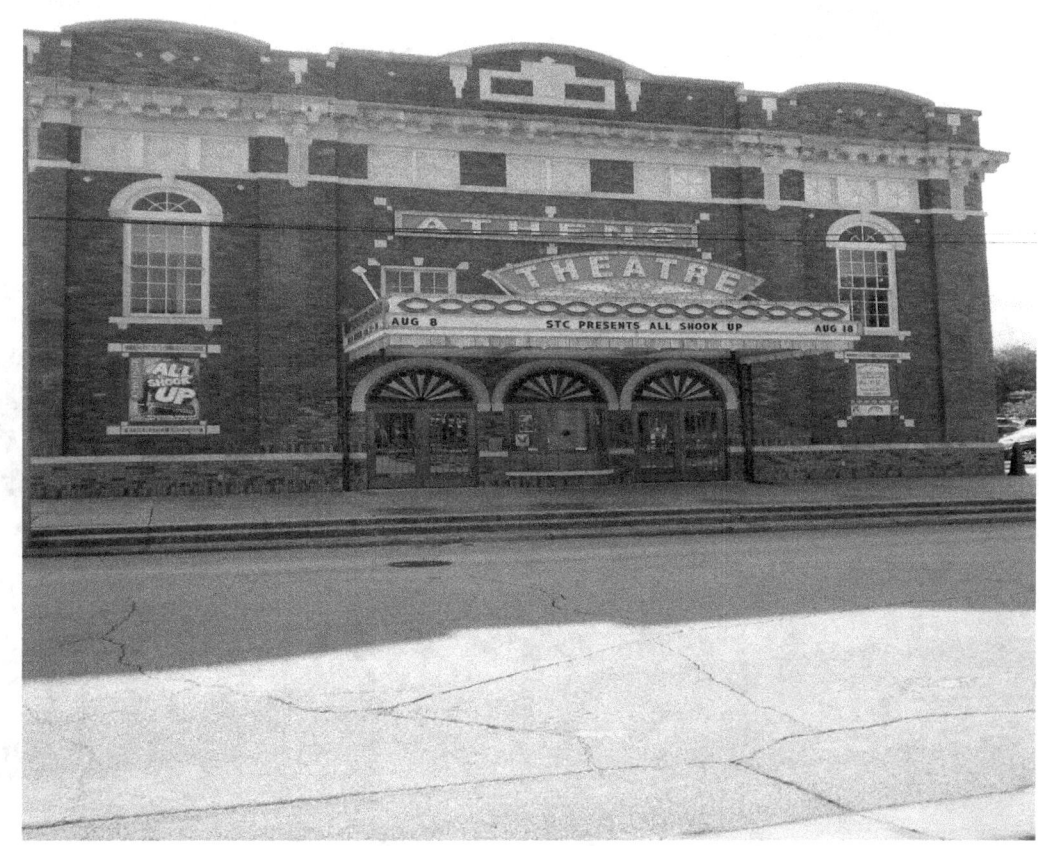

Deland Radio Control Club

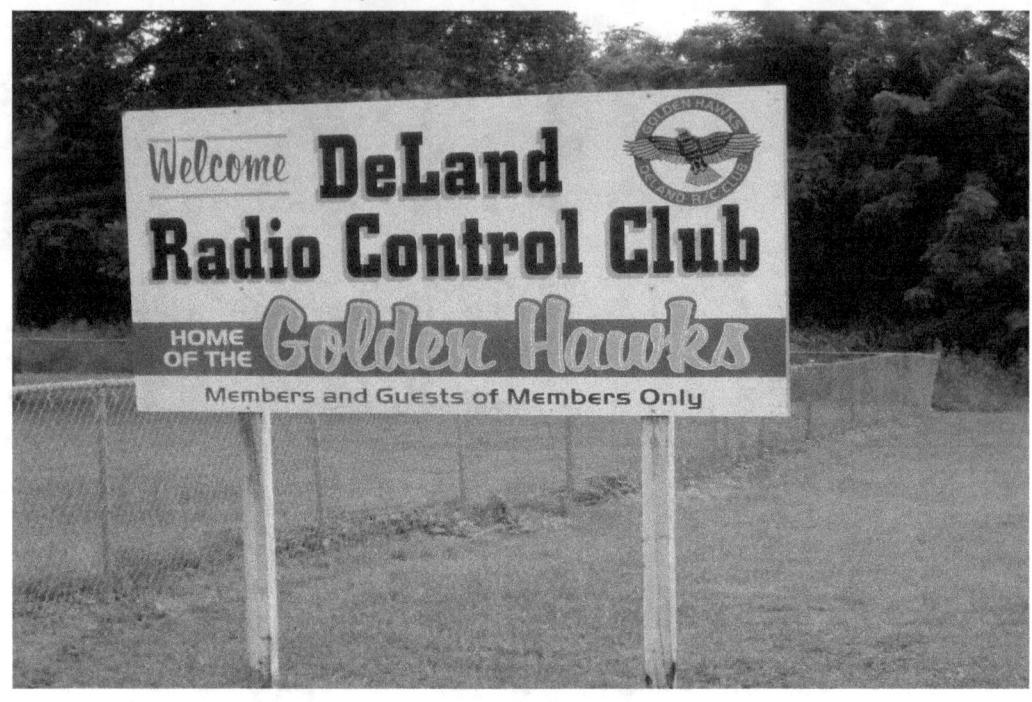

Sperling Sports Complex

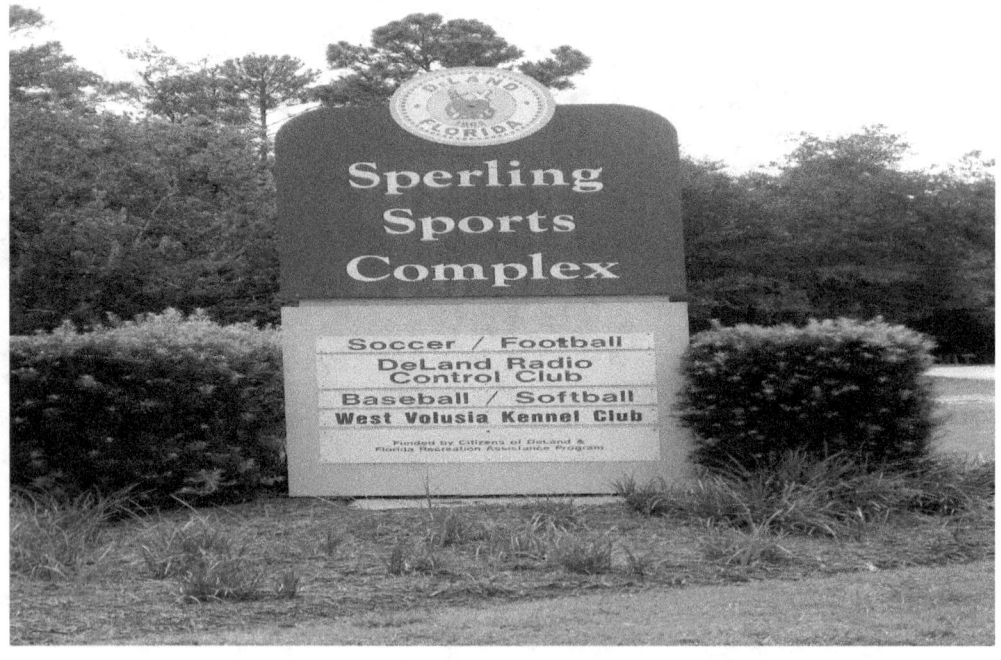

DeLand Family YMCA

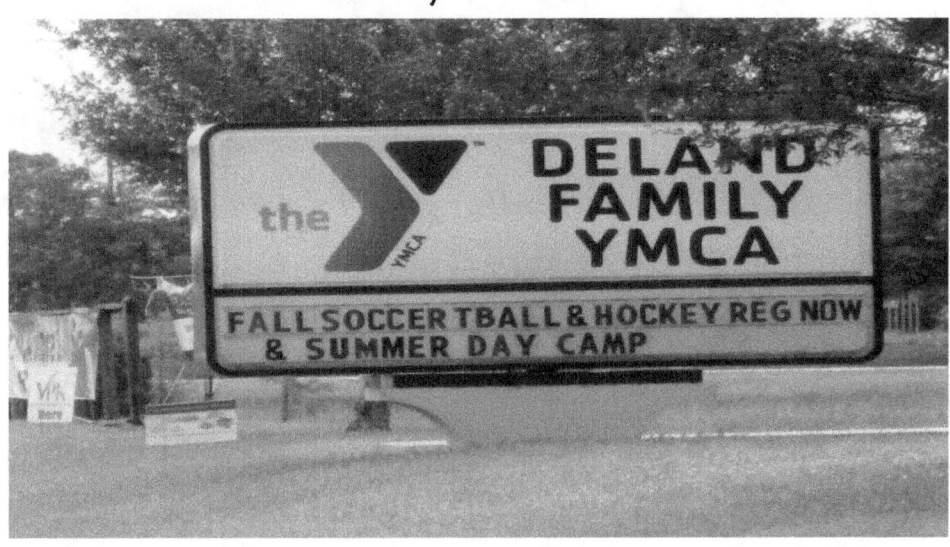

Museum of Florida Art

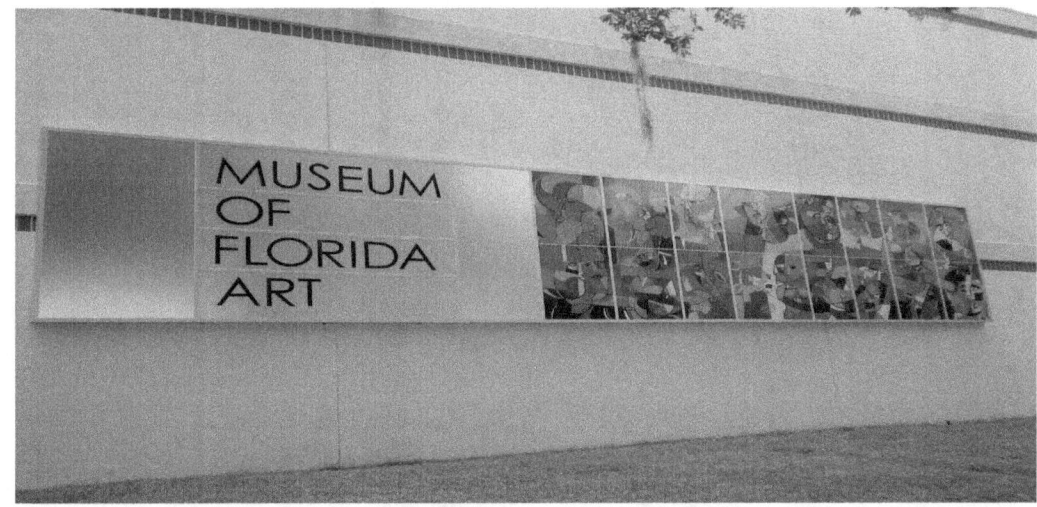